Little Red Hen Mak

MW01040161

2 "What could we do?" asked Rabbit.

"We could make soup," said Little Red Hen.

"Who could find some carrots?"
asked Little Red Hen.

"I could!" said Rabbit.

"Who could find some green beans?"
asked Little Red Hen.

"I could find green beans," said Duck.

"Who could find some potatoes?"
asked Little Red Hen.

"I could find potatoes," said Dog.

"Who could find some corn?"
asked Little Red Hen.

"I could find some corn," said Cow.

The carrots go into the pot.

The green beans go into the pot. 13

The potatoes and the corn
go into the pot.

"Who could eat some soup?"
asked Little Red Hen.

15

"We could!" said Rabbit, Duck, Dog, and Cow.

"Mmmm! Yummy vegetable soup."